Black Panther

A Fun and Educational Book for Kids with Amazing Facts and Pictures

Publisher information Odette Leo

Contact Info@OdetteLeo.be

Author Odette Leo

Table of Contents

Introduction

The phrase "Black Panther" refers to a melanistic (dark-colored) variation of numerous different species, such as leopards, jaguars, and cougars, rather than a specific type of animal. A genetic mutation that results in an excess of melanin, which gives the fur its dark color, is the reason of the black colour.

In many regions of the world, including Africa, Asia, and the Americas, black panthers are typically found in dense jungles and forested areas. They are sly predators with a reputation for power, agility, and speed. They are not all black, despite their dark coloring; a close examination of their fur frequently reveals subtle patches or patterns.

The hunting of black panthers for their fur, which is highly prized in some cultures, and habitat degradation are only two of the many problems they face. To preserve the survival of these majestic animals in the wild, however, protection measures are being taken.

Scientific Name

Depending on the species, the Black Panther has a different scientific name. Panthera pardus is the scientific term for the Black Panther subspecies of the leopard, whereas Panthera onca is the name for the Black Panther subspecies of the jaguar. Black versions of other big cat species, such as the cougar (Puma concolor) or the serval, can also be referred to as "black panthers" (Leptailurus serval).

Appearance

The melanistic coloring of black panthers, which is brought on by a genetic abnormality that causes an excess of melanin to be produced, gives them a distinctive appearance. Although they are sometimes characterized to as "black," in reality they are a very dark shade of brown or grey, and a close examination of their fur frequently reveals faint patches or patterns.

Black panthers have many physical traits with their non-melanistic relatives, such as powerful jaws, keen claws, and muscular bodies. They are typically larger than the other individuals in their species, presumably as a result of the melanistic gene's link to higher stature. Also well-known for their keen hearing and vision, black panthers hunt prey like deer, wild boar, and small mammals.

Depending on the species, black panthers have different distinct appearances. Black panthers of the jaguar species, for instance, have stockier builds and shorter legs than their leopard counterparts. But, what distinguishes black panthers from other big cats is their common melanistic coloring.

Geography

Africa, Asia, and the Americas are just a few of the places in the world where black panthers can be found. Their dark coloring serves as camouflage and makes them better hunters in the deep forests and jungles where they frequently reside.

Black panthers may usually be found in the tropical jungles of nations like Kenya, Tanzania, and Cameroon in Africa. They can be found in Asia in nations including India, Nepal, and Indonesia. Black panthers may be found throughout Central and South America, which includes nations like Mexico, Brazil, and Peru.

Depending on the species, different areas are home to black panthers. A large portion of sub-Saharan Africa, for instance, is home to black panthers of the leopard species, but black panthers of the jaguar species are found in South and Central America, as well as some regions of the southern United States. Yet, because of their dark coloring, black panthers can be challenging to see and study in the wild, making it impossible to determine their exact range.

Behavior

Because their behavior is mostly influenced by their species, black panthers exhibit comparable behavioral characteristics to their non-melanistic counterparts. The stealth and agility of black panthers, on the other hand, are what they use to hunt prey and elude predators.

Black panthers are reclusive creatures that only socialize with other black panthers during mating season. Due to their territorial nature, they will scrape trees and urinate to identify their territory. Due to their nocturnal nature, black panthers are most active in the early morning and late evening.

Black panthers are expert hunters, and they frequently track their prey from the shadows before striking unexpectedly. They can hunt fish and other water animals and have good swimming abilities.

Black panthers are challenging to examine in the field since they are frequently located in tangled forests and jungles. Yet, using video traps and other monitoring methods, scientists have been able to study their activities. Black panthers are a vital component of their ecosystems and play a significant role in controlling the populations of other animals, despite their elusiveness.

Reproduction

Similar to their non-melanistic cousins, black panthers reproduce differently depending on the species. Black panthers typically attain sexual maturity between the ages of 2-3 and will only mate at specified periods of the year.

Black Panther mating can persist for many days and typically takes place during the rainy season when prey is more plentiful. During a gestation of roughly 90-110 days, females will give birth to a litter of typically 2-3 cubs.

Black Panther females feed their pups for several months and are in charge of caring for and rearing them. The mother will educate the cubs how to hunt and survive in the wild after they have been weaned. Around 1-2 years old, young black panthers usually depart from their mother to find their own territory.

Black panthers play a crucial role in maintaining the balance of other animal species in their environments. It is crucial to safeguard these wonderful animals and their habitats since habitat degradation and poaching have endangered many Black Panther populations.

Social Life

Black panthers do not form social groupings like some other big cat species and are often solitary creatures. Their own territories, which can range in size depending on the availability of prey and other resources, are established and defended by them.

Black panthers may contact with other members of their species during mating season, despite the fact that they are solitary animals. Males will roam throughout this time in search of receptive females, and they may compete with one another for the chance to mate.

Black Panther females are in charge of taking care of and raising their young, and they normally accomplish this by themselves. Following weaning, the cubs will start to learn how to hunt and survive without their mother. Eventually, they will depart from her to create their own territory.

Black panthers contribute significantly to their ecosystems and are an essential link in the food chain, despite the fact that they may not have a complicated social structure like some other animals. Maintaining healthy ecosystems and preserving these amazing animals for future generations depend on protecting their habitats and populations.

Habitat

Due to their adaptability, black panthers can live successfully in a wide range of habitats, including deep forests, jungles, swamps, and even desert regions. Yet, depending on the species, they may have certain habitat preferences.

Sub-Saharan Africa is home to leopard black panthers, which favor dry woodlands, montane forests, and rainforests. They can adapt to live in environments with a high human presence and are also found in savannas and grasslands.

Black panthers, often known as jaguars, are native to Central and South America and enjoy marshes and dense tropical rainforests. Scrublands and meadows also contain them.

Asia, encompassing India, Nepal, and Southeast Asia, is home to black panthers. Asiatic black panthers' preferred environment varies depending on the species, however they are often found in wooded areas.

Black Panther populations are seriously threatened by habitat loss, fragmentation, and degradation brought on by human activities including deforestation, agriculture, and urbanization. To safeguard their habitats and guarantee the survival of these amazing animals, conservation activities are required.

Senses

Due to their keen senses, black panthers are able to survive in the wild. They depend significantly on their senses of sight, hearing, and smell, like other large cats do, to hunt prey and evade predators.

Their retinas are protected by a layer of cells known as the tapetum lucidum, which also gives them exceptionally keen eyesight and superb night vision. This layer allows them to see in low light because it bounces light back through the retina.

Also, because to their highly developed hearing, they are able to detect distant sounds such as the movements of prey or the approach of a predator. They can identify possible prey, mark their territory, and stay safe thanks to their keen sense of smell.

Black panthers have vibrissae on their faces, which are particularly sensitive to touch in addition to their other senses. These whiskers aid them in low-light navigation and have the ability to detect minute changes in air currents that might alert them to the presence of prey or predators.

Black panthers are formidable predators in the wild due to their highly developed senses, which enable them to traverse their surroundings and hunt successfully.

Feeding

The main sources of food for black panthers, which are carnivores, include deer, wild boar, monkeys, birds, and smaller mammals like rabbits and rodents. As opportunistic hunters, they will also consume carrion if it is present.

Black panthers are expert hunters who pursue and ambush their victims using their strong senses. They have a reputation for being strong and agile, which enables them to pounce on larger prey. They frequently hunt at night or in dimly lit areas where their prey may be less vigilant.

Black panthers usually drag their prey to a remote location once they catch it so they can eat it. The nutrient-rich internal organs, such as the liver and heart, will be consumed first. In order to protect it from scavengers, they could also bury their prey before returning to it later to resume feeding.

To maintain their energy levels and muscle strength, black panthers need a diet rich in protein and fat. They can conserve energy and concentrate on hunting for their next meal by

relying on a single massive kill to provide sustenance for
several days.

Diet

As carnivores, black panthers mostly consume prey such as deer, wild boar, monkeys, birds, and smaller animals like rabbits and rodents. As opportunistic hunters, they will also consume carrion if it is present.

Black panthers are expert hunters who pursue and ambush their victims using their strong senses. They have a reputation for being strong and agile, which enables them to pounce on larger prey. They frequently hunt at night or in dimly lit areas where their prey may be less vigilant.

Black panthers usually drag their prey to a remote location once they catch it so they can eat it. The nutrient-rich internal organs, such as the liver and heart, will be consumed first. In order to protect it from scavengers, they could also bury their prey before returning to it later to resume feeding.

To maintain their energy levels and muscle strength, black panthers need a diet rich in protein and fat. They can conserve energy and concentrate on hunting for their next meal by

relying on a single massive kill to provide sustenance for
several days.

Babies

Like other big cats, black panthers give birth to live young. Black panthers normally go through a 90 to 105-day gestation phase. A den or cave, which is typically a secluded spot, is where the mother gives birth so she can nurse and tend to her cubs.

Black panthers typically have two to three pups in each litter, though this can vary depending on the species and the amount of food available. The mother must provide all of the cubs' needs for survival because they are born blind and defenseless.

Over several months, the mother will milk her cubs until they are strong enough to start eating solid food. She will also impart valuable hunting and survival skills to them throughout this time, including how to stalk prey and stay safe.

After spending between 18 to 24 months with their mother, the cubs will eventually grow independent and start to define their own territories. Female cubs may remain in the same region and eventually set up their own territories nearby, however male cubs often leave their mother's territory and create their own.

Black panthers reach sexual maturity between the ages of two and three, at which point they are able to reproduce and carry on the species' cycle of life.

Predators

Black panthers are the top predators, hence they don't have many adversaries in the wild. But, larger predators like crocodiles, pythons, and other big cats, like lions and tigers, may occasionally feast on them.

In some places, people may potentially be a threat to black panthers through habitat damage or hunting. Black panthers have been targeted in some locations for their flesh, fur, or as hunting trophies, which has led to population decreases in some places.

Black panthers are fierce predators that are generally well suited to their habitats, making them less susceptible to predation than many other species in their ecosystems. But, like all species, they are crucial to keeping the ecosystems in balance, thus losing them would have a big influence on the local flora and fauna.

Evolution

Black panthers are a member of the Felidae family of big cats, and their evolution is closely related to that of the larger group of big cats. The earliest big cats are thought to have evolved around 10 million years ago, while the family Felidae is thought to have first appeared around 25 million years ago.

Instead of being a separate species, black panthers are a melanistic variation of numerous big cat species, such as leopards and jaguars. A genetic mutation that results in an excess of the melanin pigment, which gives the fur its dark hue, is what imparts the black coloration to the fur.

The cats benefit from enhanced camouflage in dense forests and increased heat absorption in colder regions because to their black coloring. In wide spaces, though, it also increases their visibility to potential prey.

Natural selection and genetic drift are only two examples of the many forces that have influenced the evolution of black panthers. Due to a combination of these reasons, various populations of black panthers have grown throughout the world, each of which has evolved to suit the unique environmental requirements of its habitat.

Overall, the genetic diversity and adaptation of black panthers are still being shaped by their ongoing evolution in response to shifting environmental stressors.

Population

Since black panthers are not a separate species but rather a melanistic variation of leopards and jaguars, it is challenging to quantify their population. However, habitat destruction, poaching, and conflicts between people and wildlife are putting the populations of these big cats in general at risk.

Leopards are categorized as a "vulnerable" species by the International Union for Conservation of Nature (IUCN), with populations decreasing in many regions as a result of habitat loss and fragmentation, hunting, and retaliatory killing by people. With population declines brought on by habitat loss and fragmentation, poaching, and conflicts with humans, jaguars are also considered to be "near endangered."

Although it is unknown how many black panthers there are in the wild, it is believed that their numbers are falling along with those of their parent species. These animals and their habitats are being safeguarded by conservation efforts, which include the creation of protected areas and conservation programs aimed at minimizing conflicts between people and wildlife and fostering sustainable resource use.

Ultimately, it is crucial to protect black panthers and their parent species for the wellbeing and diversity of the ecosystems in which they inhabit, as well as to ensure the survival of these iconic animals.

Conservation Status

Because black panthers are a melanistic variation of leopards and jaguars rather than a separate species, their conservation status is correlated with that of their parent species.

The International Union for Conservation of Nature (IUCN) Red List has designated leopards as "vulnerable," with numbers decreasing in many regions as a result of habitat loss, fragmentation, and degradation, as well as poaching, retaliatory killing, and confrontations with humans.

The IUCN has classified jaguars as "near threatened," with numbers dwindling as a result of habitat loss and fragmentation, hunting, and conflicts with people.

Black panthers and their parent species have key roles as apex predators and help to control the numbers of other animals in their environments, making their protection essential for preserving the health and diversity of their ecosystems.

These species are being conserved through the creation of protected areas, the encouragement of sustainable resource use, and initiatives to lessen conflict between people and wildlife. Also, efforts are being made in the areas of research and monitoring to better understand the ecology and behavior of these creatures and to create conservation measures that will ensure their long-term existence.

Health

Black panthers are prone to a wide range of health problems, including infectious diseases, parasites, wounds, and genetic disorders, much like all other wild animals. The health of black panthers and their numbers may also be impacted by habitat loss and fragmentation, poaching, and other human activities.

Black panthers and other big cats are monitored for health by conservation groups, and when necessary, medical attention and treatment are given by wildlife veterinarians. This may entail keeping an eye on and controlling infectious diseases, administering immunizations and other preventative measures, and rendering emergency medical care for accidents.

Conservation initiatives prioritize preserving the health of entire populations and ecosystems in addition to controlling the health of individual animals. The main causes of threats to black panthers and their habitats, such as habitat loss, fragmentation, and degradation, as well as illicit poaching and wildlife trafficking, must be addressed in order to achieve this.

For the long-term survival of these creatures as well as the health and biodiversity of their habitats, it is essential to preserve the health of black panthers and their ecosystems.

Lifespan

Black panthers' longevity can vary based on a number of variables, including their environment, the species to which they belong, and their access to food and resources.

Big cats, such as leopards and jaguars, have an average lifespan of 12 to 15 years in the wild. Some people have been known to live for 20 years or longer, though.

Due to the availability of a steady supply of food and resources as well as access to medical treatment, black panthers and other large cats may live longer in captivity. Some black panthers kept in captivity have survived up to 25 years or more.

It's crucial to remember that a number of variables, such as habitat degradation, poaching, and conflicts between people and animals, can have an impact on the longevity of black panthers and other large cats. These creatures' chances of survival and quality of life can be improved by conservation activities targeted at safeguarding them and their habitats.

Conclusion

In conclusion, black panthers are a melanistic variation of leopards and jaguars rather than a separate species. They inhabit a variety of settings throughout their range and are distinguished by their stunning black colour. Black panthers, like its parent species, are under threat from habitat loss, poaching, and conflicts with people and other wildlife. Conservation efforts are being made to save these creatures and their ecosystems.

Black panthers' precise population size is unclear, but it is nevertheless important to protect them for the long-term sustainability and biodiversity of their habitats. The creation of protected areas, responsible resource use, and a decrease in human-wildlife conflict are all part of the conservation efforts for these creatures. In addition, efforts are being made in study and observation to better understand the ecology and behavior of these animals and to create conservation methods that will ensure their survival.

We can contribute to ensuring the survival of these iconic

animals and the health of their ecosystems for future generations by safeguarding black panthers and their parent species.

Thank you